# SPECIAL ADVENTURES WITH MY LITTLE BROTHER

## ANNIE BECKETT

◆ FriesenPress

One Printers Way
Altona, MB R0G 0B0
Canada

www.friesenpress.com

**Copyright © 2023 by Annie Beckett, BPHE, BEd**
First Edition — 2023

All rights reserved.

Illustrated by Rebecca Bender
Nicole Mclean - Editor

No part of this publication may be reproduced in any form, or by any means, electronic or mechanical, including photocopying, recording, or any information browsing, storage, or retrieval system, without permission in writing from FriesenPress.

ISBN
978-1-03-917135-0 (Hardcover)
978-1-03-917134-3 (Paperback)
978-1-03-917136-7 (eBook)

1. JUVENILE NONFICTION, SOCIAL TOPICS, SPECIAL NEEDS

Distributed to the trade by The Ingram Book Company

This book is dedicated to my wonderful husband
and two beautiful boys, and to my parents
for their unwavering love and support.

I am a big brother and **THOMAS** is my little brother. We are family. Thomas and I do lots of important work together. We are very busy—come check us out!

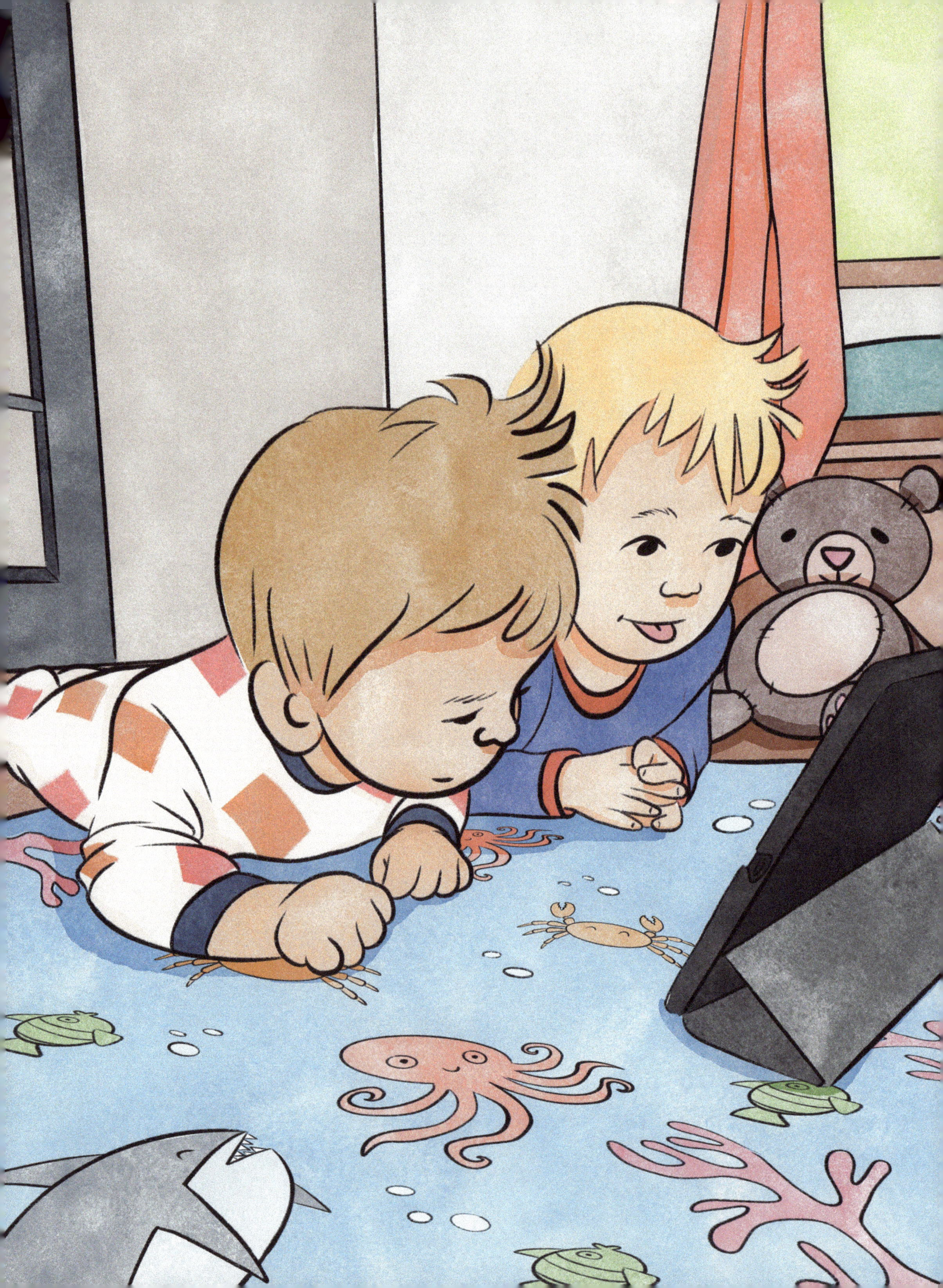

It is tummy time! We watch our shows while we make our muscles BIG! How about this show, **THOMAS**?

---
*Daily therapy helps strengthen underdeveloped muscle groups (hypoplasia), helps compensate for those who have low muscle tone (hypotonia), and improves functional mobility and overall health.*

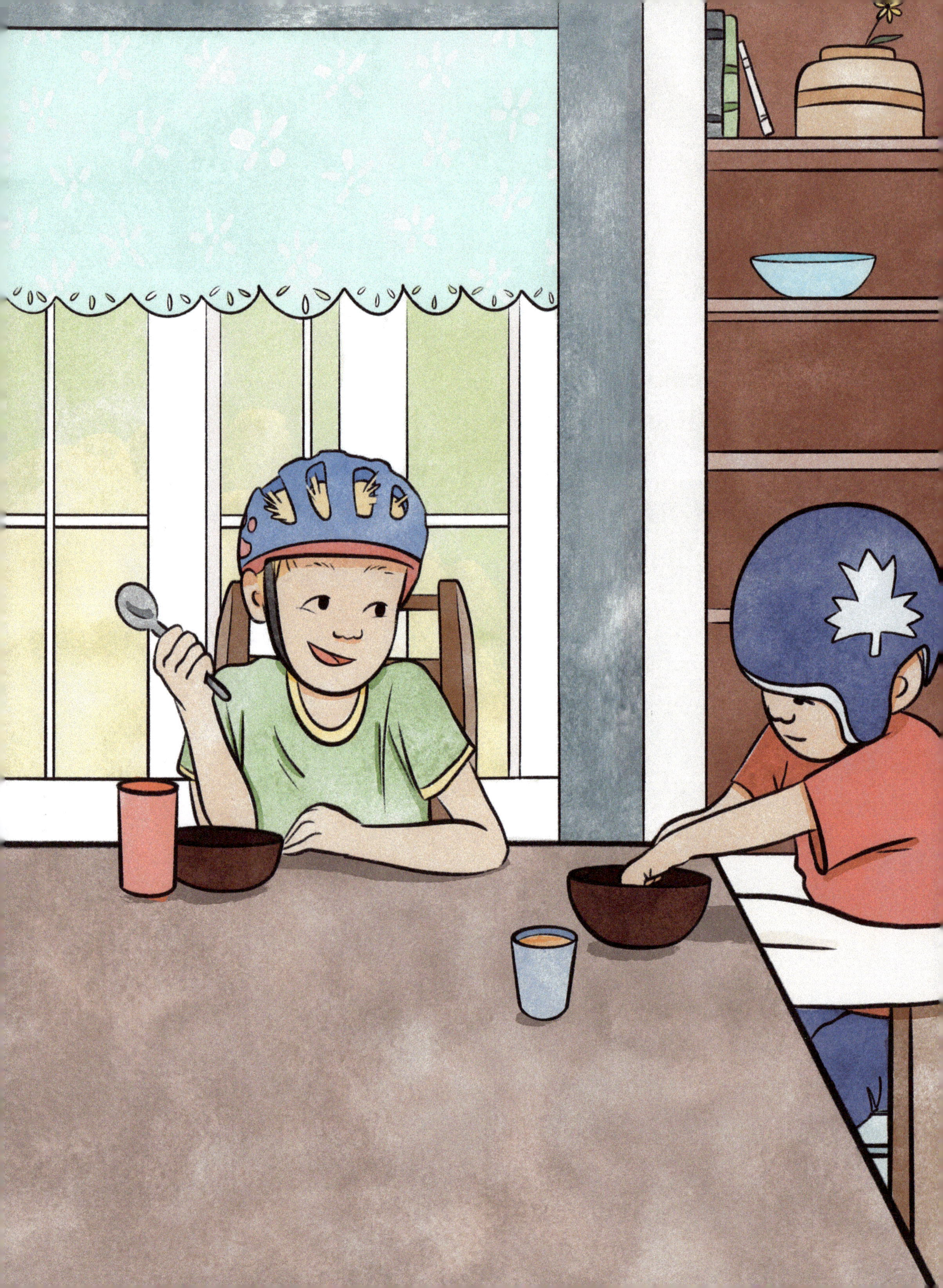

We wear our helmets together at breakfast time. After breakfast, we will go to the park to ride our motorcycles.

---
A cranial remolding helmet is sometimes worn for approximately 3-5 months during the newborn stage to correct a flat spot that formed on the skull. Flat spots result from infants' heads resting against firm surfaces—like car seats or mattresses—for prolonged periods of time. The limited mobility of infants affected by low muscle tone means that they are more susceptible to developing these flat spots.

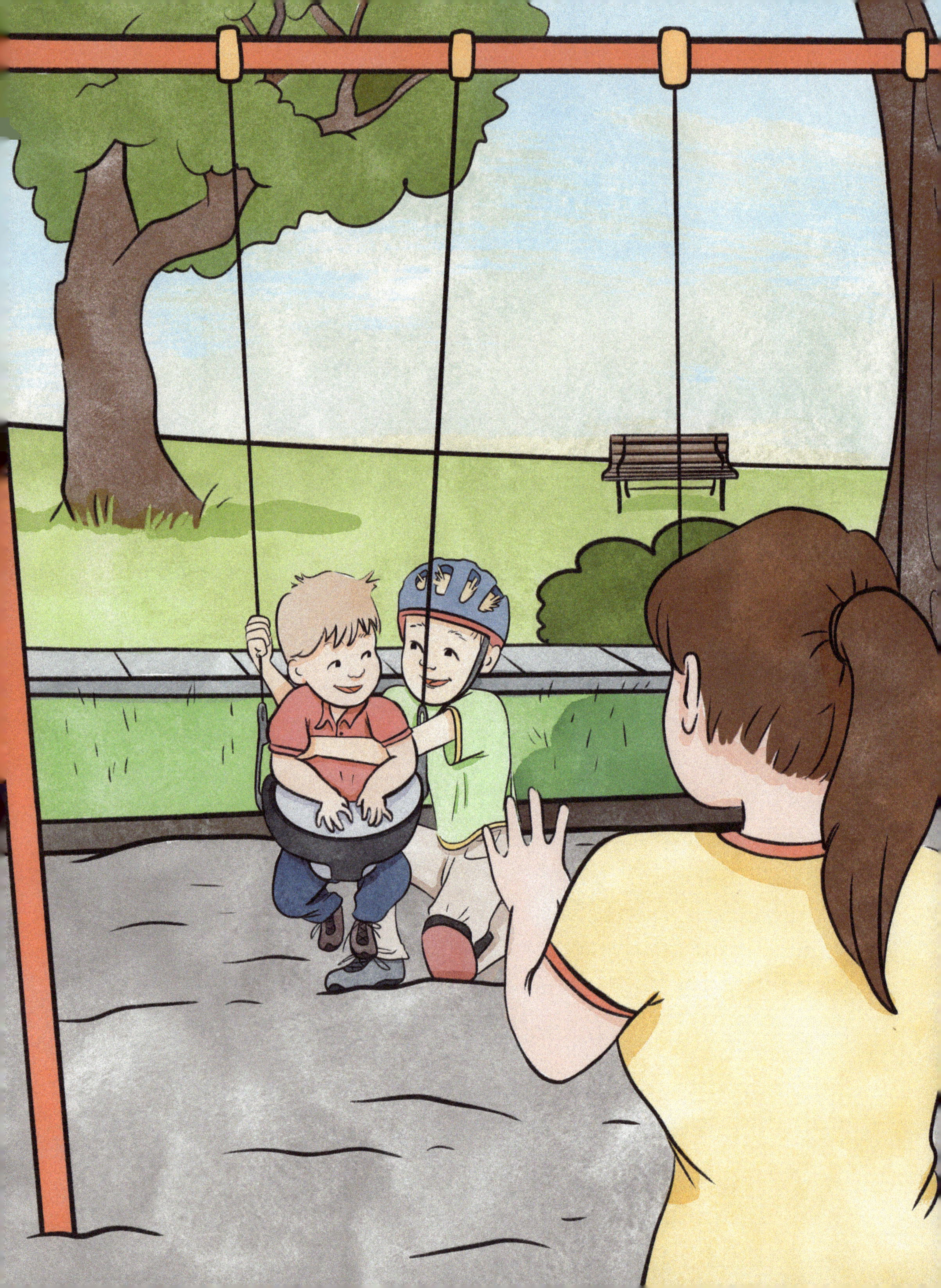

**THOMAS** loves hugs—he likes my hugs the best, though. If I hug Thomas, it makes him happy. See—**he's smiling!**

---
*A 'HuggaPod' is beneficial for a child with low muscle tone who may require more trunk support in assisted seating positions or swings.*

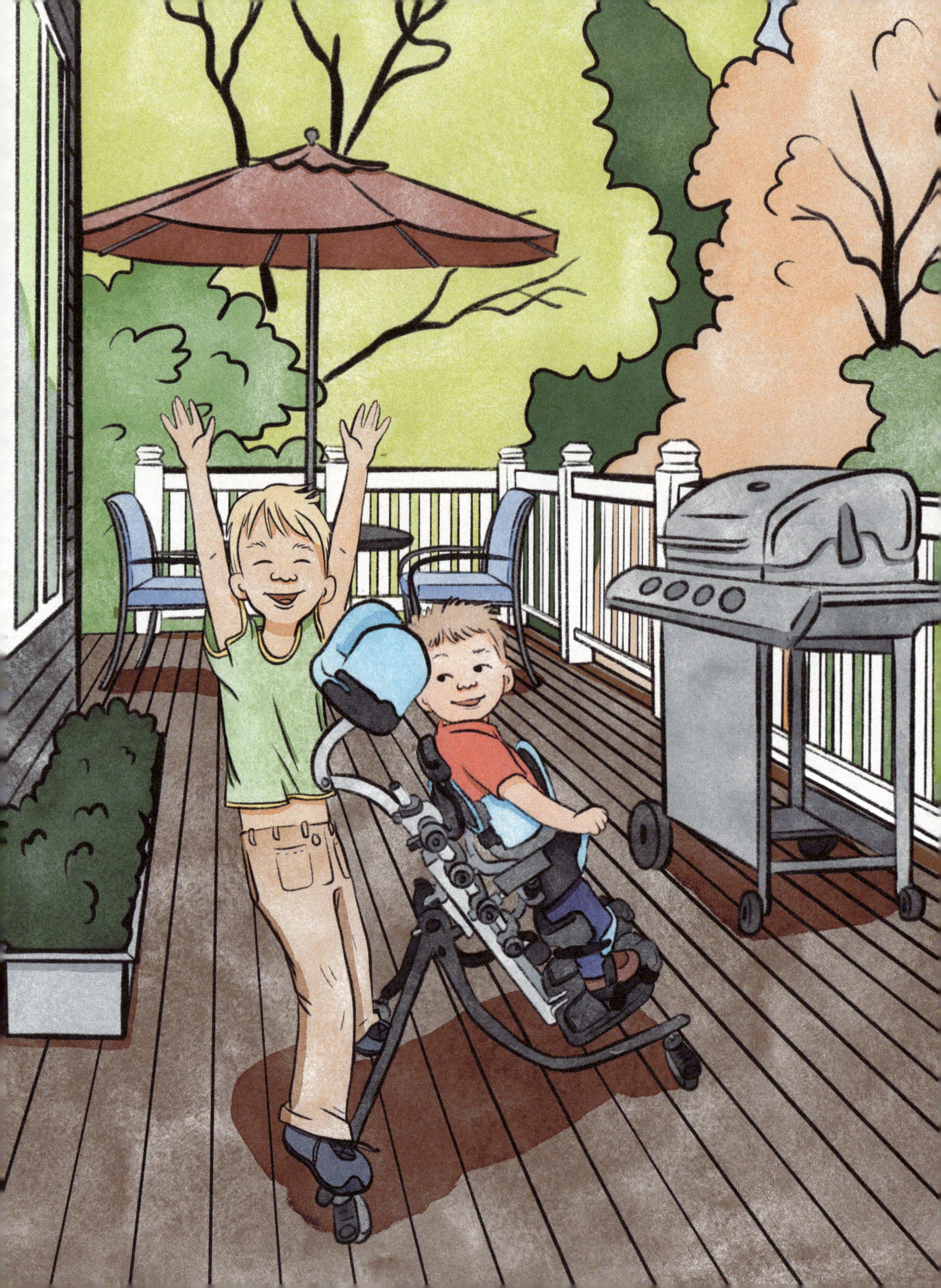

Now we need to go for a ride in the robot!
**Faster, THOMAS, faster!** Look—no hands!

*A stander allows for a child who may be unable to weight-bear through the legs to be in an upright posture. Weight-bearing promotes proper hip and joint development, helps prevent contractures, and reduces spasticity.*

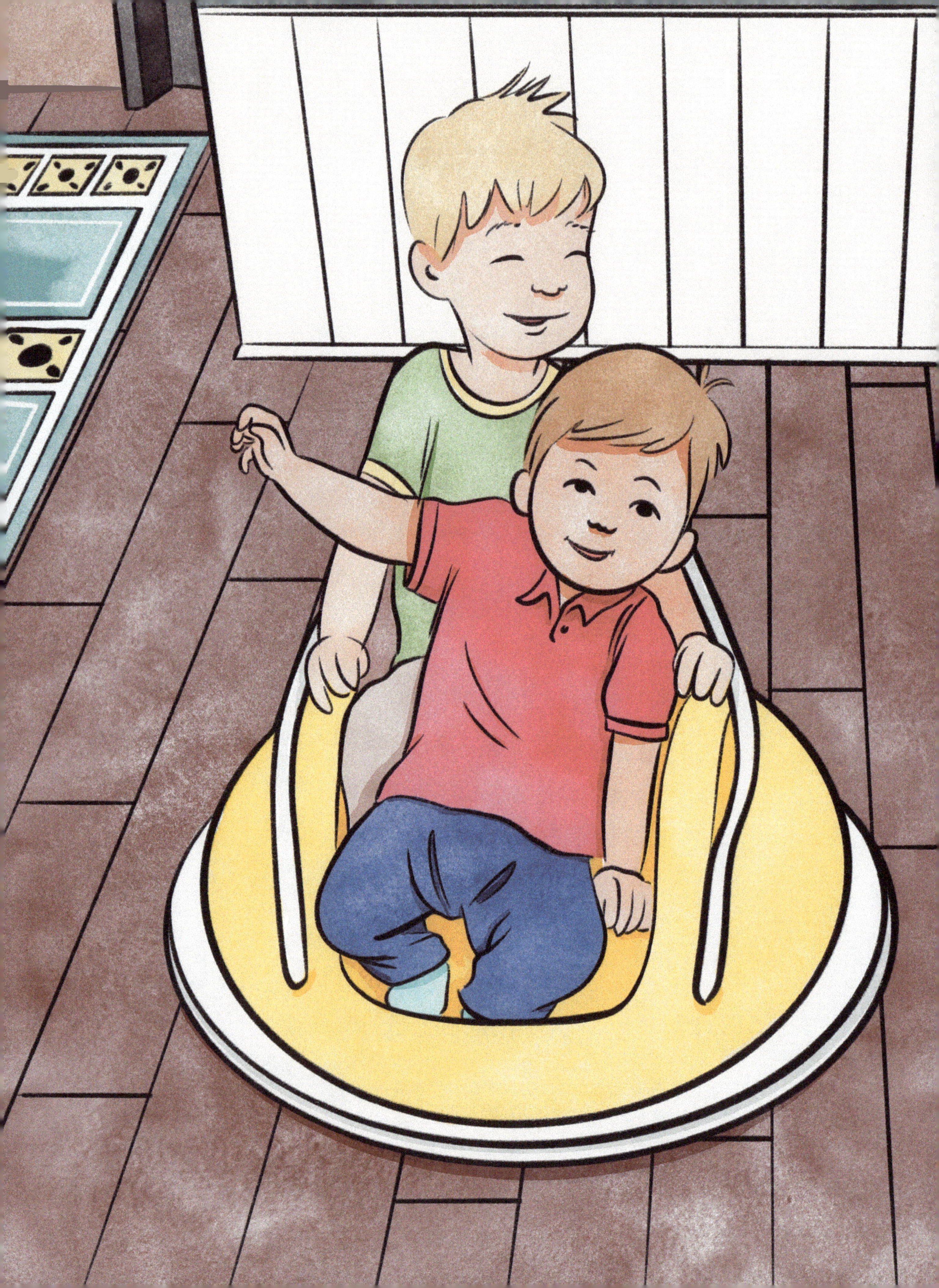

**Vroom! Vroom!** Time to catch the bad guys! Hold on tight, THOMAS!

---

*This adapted Go-Cart is a fun and safe toy which can be controlled by a caregiver using the remote control or can be controlled by a child using the built-in joystick; this allows the child to develop a greater sense of independence.*

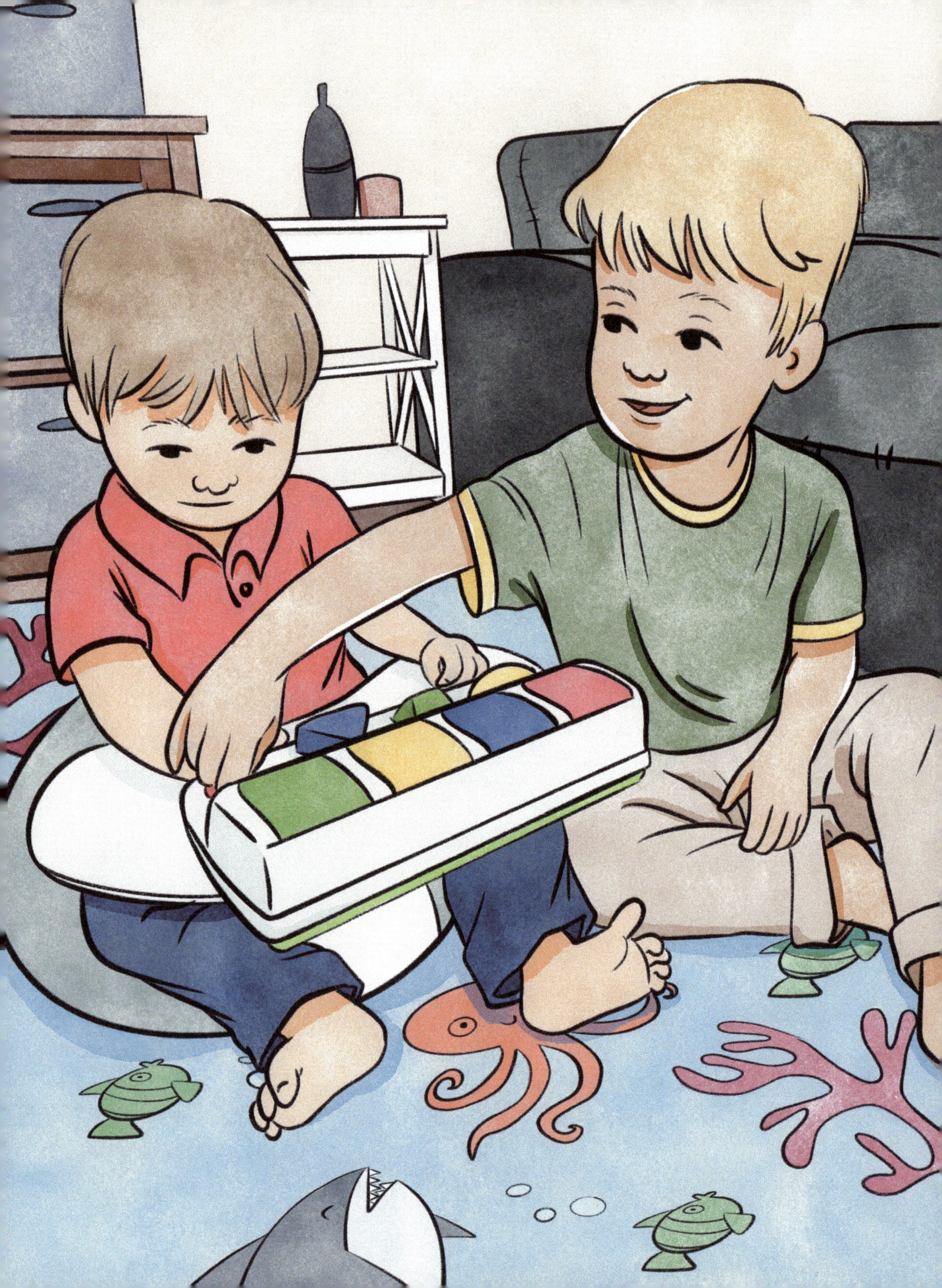

My brother is the best sharer.
Can I have this? He says yes!

---
*A person who is nonverbal has difficulty vocalizing using words; this is not to be confused with someone who is noncommunicative. Communicating a desire to share can be as simple as a smile invitation or attempting to reach for a toy.*

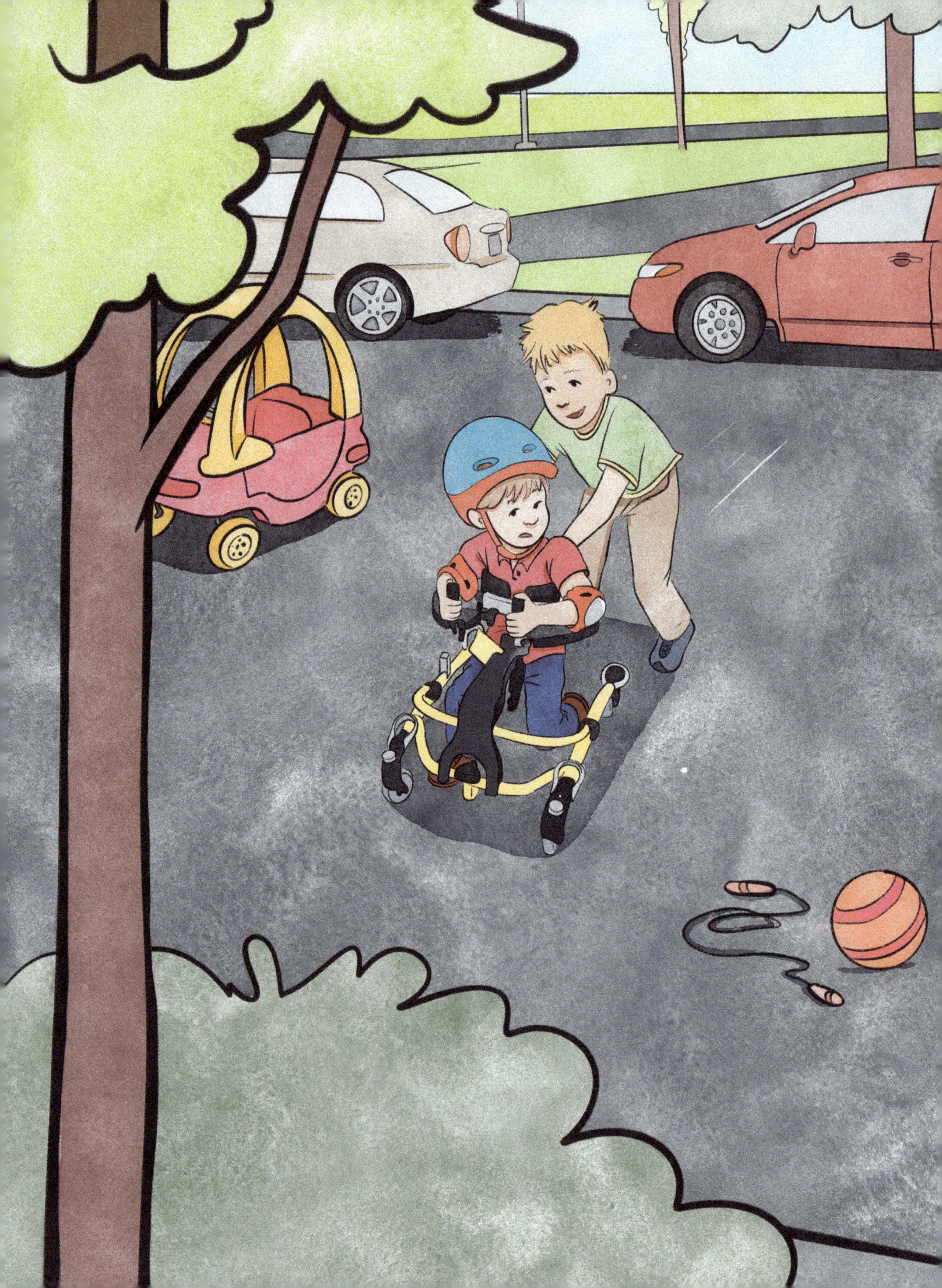

Time to put on my super jets. 1... 2... 3... Blast off! Oh no! We are about to hit the moon! Watch out, **THOMAS**! **CRASH!**

---
*A walker or gait trainer is an assisted mobility device that strengthens a child's standing and walking muscles, while also allowing them to explore their environment without depending on a caregiver for help. Research shows that walkers and gait trainers may also promote cognitive development.*

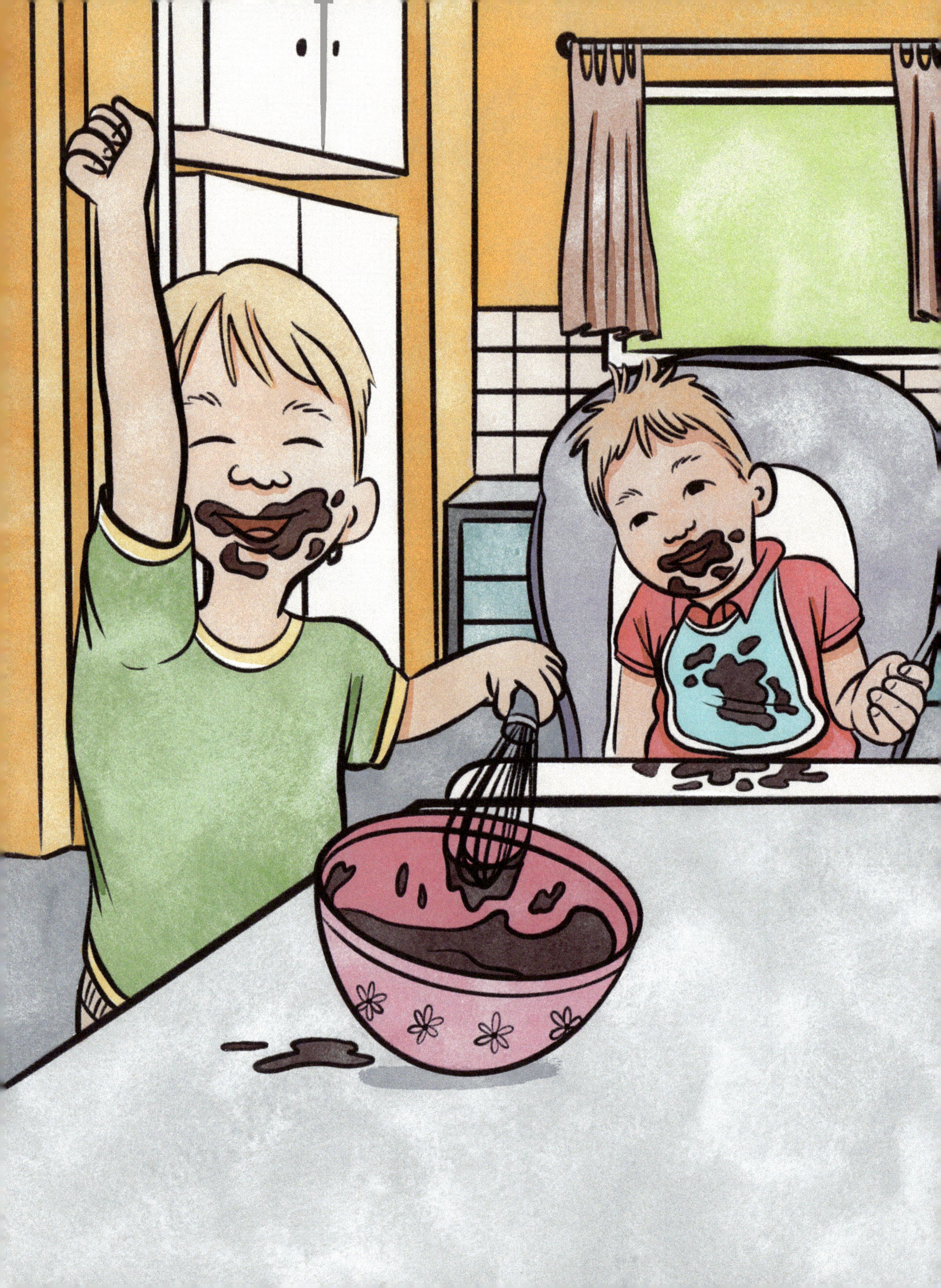

**THOMAS** loves desserts, just like me! We cheer when he eats. Having a little brother means eating all the pudding and LOTS of celebrating! **Hip, hip, hooray!**

---
*A gastrostomy tube (G-Tube) helps children who have trouble eating ensure they get the fluids and calories they need. It is inserted through the abdomen to bring nutrients directly into the stomach. It can be used to supplement oral feeding.*

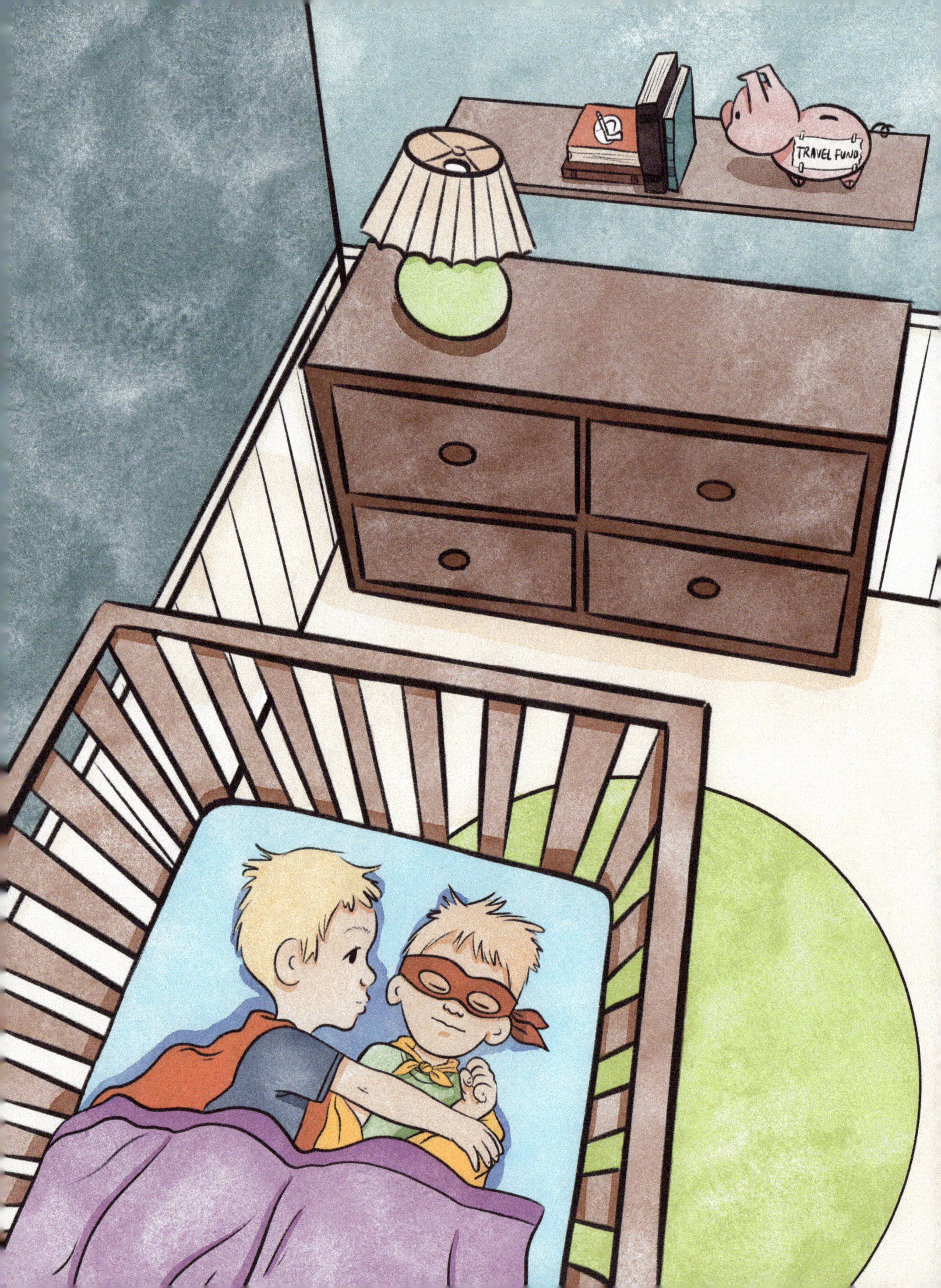
TRAVEL FUND

Mommy says no kisses on the lips, or I will spread germs. He likes it when I kiss his forehead. Goodnight, THOMAS! **I love you.** I can't wait for tomorrow's special adventures!

---
*Some people with genetic conditions are immunocompromised; this means they have a weakened immune system, more difficulty fighting infections, and they are more likely to get sick or sustain illness for a longer period of time.*